Interview Preparation And Success Tips: A Detailed Guide on How to Answer Interview Questions and Bag That Dream Job!

© *Written By : Ernest Enabulele*

/

Table of Contents

Introduction

An interview is one of the crucial parts in a job-seeking quest. Therefore, you have to make a good impression to justify what you have in your resume. Interviews can be so tricky and worrisome if you are not prepared.

Going to an interview gives you a real chance to impress a hiring manager. There's no guarantee about what you'll be asked, but it would be great to know there are a number of questions that come up again and again.While we unfortunately can't read minds, it's important that you have powerful answers to these questions to help you make a big impact.

This book will be your step-by-step guide to interview confidence, eliminate that feeling of anxiety and ultimately help you to secure your next job, by giving you the tools to answer interview questions better than other candidates.Knowing what the interviewer wants to hear and being able to deliver the prefect answer gives you a huge advantage over any other candidates that will be interviewed.

Chapter 1: Interview Preparation

Your Definitive Guide to Interviews

Interviews are inevitable part of job hunting but they don't need to be something you dread. With the right amount of preparation you can stand out from the other candidates and give yourself a much better chance of getting that job.

Here is my tried and tested guide for interviews:

✓ Ask

If the letter inviting you to an interview is rather vague, don't just accept it. It will be time to ask some questions, so give HR a call and ask for a few more details. It's advisable to have names and job titles of your interviewer(s) and what the interview agenda will be. Get as many facts as you can since all information will help you focus in the right areas for your interview. The added bonus for requesting this information is that the HR department will remember your high level of professionalism which will give them a very good first impression of you.

Always prepare at least 3 questions to ask at your interview. These should be appropriate to the role or to the company - but don't try and be clever in asking a question to catch out your interview panel, it will put them right off you. Good question areas are: the products and/or services provided by the company, training procedures and career progression.

If you think you have the confidence to ask questions during the interview as opposed to just at the end please do so, it will demonstrate you are engaged in the interview process and are interested in the role. Take care not to interrupt the interviewer with your questions though, always be patient and let them finish talking before jumping in.

✓ Body language

Even if you are nervous, anxious or scared out of your wits, a positive body language will do you well and boost your confidence no end. A firm handshake, an honest smile, holding your head high and shoulders back and making eye contact, will all be remembered by the interviewers as you being a positive and likable candidate.

You may want to take notice of some of your habits you have when you are nervous or being slightly economical with the truth, for example, picking your nails, fiddling with your hair, rubbing your nose, scratching your face etc. The interviewers may not pick up on what these habits represent, but it will definitely distract them. Its better that they listen to what you have to say as opposed to being mesmerised by how often you stick your finger in your ear!

✓ CV

Ensure you have a copy of your up-to-date CV with you at the interview. It is unlikely you will need to refer to it, but it will make you feel more confident having it with you. Make sure you are well versed on your CV; there is nothing worse than trying to remember where you worked 5 years ago and fumbling around in your head to recall what you did.

✓ Dipping

If you find yourself in a situation where the interview has dipped and the mood has taken a down turn - stay calm. Humour can help here but don't go too crazy, just put on a smile and explain how nervous you are and be positive. Take a deep breath and carry on. Showing your honesty and the appreciation of the situation with a positive spin will be acknowledged and appreciated by your interviewer(s). Remember there is nothing wrong in saying you are nervous, they are probably nervous too.

✓ Enthusiasm

If there is one thing I enforce more than anything else is this: be enthusiastic about the job! Even if it sounds like the dullest job on the planet, you can still show enthusiasm. Enthusiasm is highly infectious and it's something that companies cannot train. Given the choice between 2 candidates - one with skills and no enthusiasm and one with hardly any experience and bags of energy and enthusiasm -

the job will mostly likely be offered to the enthusiastic candidate. Remember: companies are happy to invest time in training for the job role, they won't want to bother training someone to have a positive attitude.

✓ Friendly

It is important that the interviewers realise that you will fit in with the team or department. Showing you are approachable and friendly is just as important as having a strong skills set in the job itself.

✓ Grooming

Yes first impressions do count. Ensure you have the simplest of things sorted: Clean polished shoes, freshly laundered and ironed clothes. If you are a smoker avoid having a quick ciggie right before the interview as the smell will linger, if you are desperate though, make sure you have mints or mouth freshener to hand. Avoid very tight fitting clothes or clothes that will irritate you.

Ladies: Take care on the jewellery and make-up, a classic look is best.Avoid showing to much skin even on a hot day.Make sure there are no holes in tights/stockings and it's always a good idea to pack a spare pair discretely in your bag - just in case.

Gentlemen: Ensure your aftershave is not going to knock out a rhino at 20 paces; less is best. Facial hair is OK as long as it's neat and tidy. Avoid 'builder's cleavage' when you bend down, so ensure your shirt is tucked in well.

✓ Homework

Make sure you have done your research on the company and the role as much as you can. Try and remember a few facts about the company, as it will be highly likely they will ask a few questions in this area at the start of the interview. By making a little effort in your research, you will gain a lot of head way at the interview.

✓ Intuition

Your preparation can in some instances go against you, especially if you have done prep work weeks in advance of the interview. Be ready to be intuitive with your answers and tweak your responses accordingly, rather than regurgitating what you have rehearsed and sounding like a robot.

✓ Killer skill set

Don't just think of qualifications and experience when preparing for your interview, chances are you will have a fabulous skill set too. It is very usual for all of us to play down what we do so well. If you made a list of all your skills most, if not all, would be transferable to anything you decide to do.

Remember soft skills are just as important as hands-on skills. So if you are an excellent negotiator, good listener, a natural leader or you just have the ability to brighten a persons day, then remember to mention this and prepare examples where you can illustrate your excellent talents.

✓ Luck

A number of people may insist that getting the job is more about luck than it is about anything else. I don't agree, if you have done your preparation, dressed according, have a positive attitude with lots of enthusiasm you will definitely be short listed or better still offered the role.

✓ Money

Unless asked, refrain from asking about money/salary or any other job perks at the interview. If you are asked any salary related questions by the interviewer, then by all means answer appropriately. What you want to avoid is to be seen as only wanting the job for the money. Even in a sales environment where salary and bonuses are a huge motivating factor; interest in the company and product are vitally important and are very appreciated.

✓ Nerves

We all get nervous prior to an interview even the interviewers. Nerves are good, it means adrenalin is pumping which will help you focus and think on your feet. Avoid using negative coping mechanisms such a drugs and alcohol to calm your nerves. Instead, you can look to Bach natural flower remedies, deep breathing exercises or positive affirmations to help you feel really confident.

✓ Openness

Especially to other people's opinions. This is particularly important if you are in a group interview setting and you have to deal with other people's opinions as well as your own. It is important to be able to express yourself without alienating others.

With certain interview techniques, some very emotive questions may be asked just to see how you react. Be honest but fair and if in doubt use something like the 'sandwich technique' where you say something positive prior to saying something controversial (or negative) and then follow up with something positive or neutral at the end. This will ensure the interviewers are under no illusion that you can handle opinions in a balanced way.

✓ Preparation

Like all things in life, preparation is key to success. Please don't go into an interview thinking you can wing-it!

You may want to consider some of the following:

> ✓ Working out the travel times to the place of interview
> ✓ Research on the company and position

- ✓ Presentation (if required)
- ✓ Your interview questions to ask interviewers
- ✓ Clothes and shoes
- ✓ Getting a good night sleep the night before
- ✓ Eating something at least 30 minutes prior to the interview
- ✓ Keeping hydrated (good for the brain)

Resist

Resist the urge to tell the interviewer(s) your whole life story. Nerves can play havoc with self censorship and you might feel the urge to share that really 'funny' story when you were really drunk on B52 cocktails in Turkey and ended up at a nightclub waving your pants in the air.

Resist the urge to be really, really honest, saying that you only want the job is because you need something to pay the bills, this is not acceptable.

Resist moaning and complaining especially about your previous or current employers (or role). Warning! Many industries are small, and the chances of your interviewer knowing someone at your old or current place of work is very likely - so you could find your self slagging-off their best friend.

- ✓ Smile

Smiling instantly builds rapport with the interviewers, and don't be put off if they don't smile back. You may have found yourself in an old fashioned interview technique of god cop - bad cop. Ensure your smile is genuine - a fake smile will be spotted a mile away.

✓ Take your time

Don't gabble your words and if you feel like you are rushing, then ask for a few moments to gather your thoughts or better still ask if the question could be repeated at the end of the interview so you can buy yourself some time to think.

✓ Understand what is expected of you

Will there be a test? Will there be a group interview with other candidates? Will you be interviewed by a panel of interviewers? Will you being attending a lunch etc

These are all important aspects of the interview that you know before you step into the interview....remember ask and gather the information that you need.

✓ Value who you are

High self esteem is important and body language and grooming will do well for you here. There is nothing wrong with saying how good you are at something, how successful a project was or what fabulous process you implemented in you current role.

What You Should Prepare Before an Interview For a Job

Many individuals these days are looking for interview for work opportunities because of the high rate of unemployment. We are having one of our country's toughest recessions ever. While finding a job is important for most people, competition has gotten really hard. Because the competition for jobs is fierce, you have to take steps to make sure that you're ahead of others.

In order to do really well when you interview for job opportunities, you should clearly define the kind of interview you'll be attending. Of course, you will have no way of knowing how the job interview will proceed until you're really doing it, but you will be able to prepare yourself to some degree. This guide has been written to help you see the different types of interviews you can expect.

The first contact is usually a screening interview and might be taken over the phone or in person. A representative from the company's human resources department will check the information on the job application or resume. You can expect a depth discussion involving your specific qualifications at this session.

However, during the following interview you can expect a pretty detailed discussion involving your work experience and job accomplishments. These interviews are usually conducted in person. A 2nd interview is given to applicants who applied that have met the qualifications of the position. This interview serves as an chance for you and the employer to find out whether or not you will be a good fit for the company's environment and other employees. During this meeting, you must make a good impression, because the first impression is usually a lasting impression.

Maybe the most challenging of all the interview types is a group style interview. During this kind of job interview, you and several other applicants will sit in a group and be questioned by a jury. The jury then places each of the appliers into several categories based on their answers to the questions. These categories are often leaders, followers, and team players. In order to be put in a category that suits your personality best, act as naturally as possible during the meeting.

Another type, the jury interview, also involves a panel of various interviewers. Nevertheless, only one applier will be expected to answer the questions. While this type of interview can feel very intimidating, if you remain calm, cool, and composed it can end favorably.

As you can see, each of these interview types will need a completely different mentality from you. For instance, in order to do well during a group interview, try to show the panel that not only are you a team player, but you connect well to other people. On the other hand, while participating in a panel type interview it's up to you only to point out each of your qualifications and skills that distinctly make you the proper person for the job. Make sure you're prepared to make any adjustments that may be needed so you shine regardless of the interview setting you walk into.

There are several particular aspects of an interview that will apply to every form of interview that you need to master before entering any interview. To prepare yourself for any interview, check everything you can about the company you're applying at. You can expect to be interviewed or tested involving your knowledge of the company. When you can answer these questions, not only will you show the interviewer that you have a real interest in securing the position, but you'll have made an impression as being brilliant and well informed.

The following thing you need to do to properly prepare yourself is to make sure you really know yourself. You will likely be questioned about your strengths and weaknesses. The interviewer will want to hear about your education, experience, skills, and talents. Don't be surprised if you're asked about you interests and hobbies during an interview. It helps to make a list about yourself and work them into a short speech that can be used to answer these types of questions. By taking the time to do this before your interview, you will be confident and well prepared for anything they might expect and sound well polished when you respond.

The 3rd step you should take when preparing for an interview is practicing answering questions. Ask a friend or family member to pose as an interviewer and have them ask you a series of questions. During this exercise you should take note of your body language, the clearness of your replies, and the amount of eye contact you do with the interviewer. It is also helpful to practice both roles, the interviewee and the interviewer, in front of a mirror.

The next factor to consider when preparing for an interview is your appearance. You absolutely must pay close attention to your appearance, all the way from your head to your toes. Regardless of what other people might believe, you will be judged based on your attire and your overall appearance. Before you walk into the interview make sure you're totally prepared. Since your appearance is important when you interview for job opportunities, you should practice good hygiene and be sure you're dressed appropriately.

One last point to keep in mind is body language. You should strive to develop a comfortable rapport with the interviewer by appearing calm and collected, but be careful not to look really laid back. Be careful about crossing your arms across your chest and avoiding eye contact, as these things can be considered negatively. By properly preparing yourself prior to a job interview you can drastically increase your chances of landing the job.

Videotaping - A Highly Effective Interview Preparation Tool

Videotaping one's self is an effective method being used more commonly for a number of business-related purposes. Even business schools are promoting the use of such a technique when trying to effectively build one's speaking abilities or presentation style. But this is not the only area in which this technique is used. Career consultants and recruiters will tell you that the best way to see how you come across in an interview is to film yourself, review the tape and continue to film and review until you like what you see (and thus, what the interviewer sees).

While videotaping yourself is a proven method for successful interviewing, it is a little more complex than simply pulling out your camera. Here I will provide you with some tricks of the trade, from setting up the camera to what you should discuss to things which you should avoid.

✓ Getting Ready

The first thing you'll want to do it set up a video camera roughly 5 to 7 feet away from the comfortable chair in which you will be sitting. Pay attention to the backdrop. You do not want to be sitting in front of a window, where the glare reflects into the camera and distorts the image, but you also do not want to have the sun facing onto you, as this will wash out your color. The perfect setting is in a room with a moderate amount of natural light as well as artificial; against a backdrop that complements the color you will be wearing is best. A white wall should always be considered as a last option. As for your attire, wearing navy or black is the best option for film.

Now, begin taping! You want to think of the camera as the interviewer, so keep eye contact at all times. The first time you do this it may seem a little unnatural, but try to relax. This is a tape that should only be seen by you, unless you are asking a friend to review (which is never a bad idea). Be as natural as possible and remember to smile. This method is only as effective as you make it, so try to get over being self-conscious and treat it like the real thing.

✓ What to Discuss

It used to be that you could easily predict the five most likely questions an interviewer was likely to ask. However, times have changed and now companies are leaning more toward questions that are classified as "behavioral."Instead of asking "Where do you see yourself in five years?" behavioral questions tempt to uncover a person's core competencies. This is achieved with questions focused on areas such as: problem solving skills, leadership challenges, communication, organization and coordination, assertiveness, creativity, goal orientation, and flexibility.

Consider questions that might be asked with regard to each of these categories. For example, a question attempting to uncover how the candidate copes with leadership challenges might be, "Recount a time when you had to deal with a difficult employee. What tactics did you use and what became of that employee?" Brainstorm questions such as these and consider and practice the answer you would give. Performing a general Internet search using the key phrase "behavioral interview" will provide you with many more potential questions.

Once you have brainstormed on what you would say, carry on a conversation with the camera as if you are being prompted with those potential questions. Ask yourself at least 5 solid questions to which you can provide a comprehensive answer. Once you've completed this step, you will also want to ask the interviewer questions in return. Brainstorming these out prior to going on camera is yet another effective preparation technique.

✓ Beware...

Here are just a couple of additional tips that will help you record a successful, videotaped interview:

When in front of the camera, keep your eye contact with the interviewer.

Don't shift your weight too much or fidget. Even as a natural part of your personality, this activity can convey several negative impressions such as insecurity, lack of interest, or inability to maintain focus.

Try to limit your hand movement. When presenting, you are told that movement of this kind is appealing and captivating to your audience, but when you are in a one-on-one situation, it can be distracting, so try to keep this to a minimum.

Performing the Self-Evaluation

The very last step in this process is the Self-Evaluation. It is crucial, no matter how painful you think it is, to review the video and note areas of improvement. Questions that you might ask include:

"Did I smile?"

"Did I maintain eye contact?"

"Where were my hands? Were they naturally in my lap or were they a featured part of the presentation?"

"Did I remember to address the interviewer by his/her name?"

"Was my speech broken? How many times did I say "Uh...?" (You need to get this down to 0).

And the most important question: "Did I seem like myself or was it a modified version of me?"

✓ Practice Makes Perfect

The key to this method is to continuing to practice so that you get to where you are comfortable presenting yourself and verbalizing your thoughts without being embarrassed or overly self-aware. The answers to the questions are only half the test in interviews. Think about it...if interviews were all about the questions and your answers, then all of them would be conducted by phone. But that's not the case because the interviewer wants to see how you "handle" the interview. And practicing by video will show you just how well you measure up.

Acing the Interview - A Guide to Landing the Job of Your Dreams!

So you got a call-back. After days of waiting anxiously by the phone, the company you submitted your resume to called and said it would like to set up a job interview. Let the heavens rejoice as you dance around the apartment you can barely afford, but thanks to the sweet little lady downstairs in the leasing office, you've been able to slip checks in two weeks late and not get caught.

But not so fast. You've got work to do. Sure the resume you labored over for months got you noticed, but that's only half the battle. You still have to close the deal by acing the interview process, and beating out even tougher competition. But have no fear. With some job interview preparation, and by following these job interview tips, you can win over your prospective employer.

1) Preparation is key. You wouldn't show up for a test without studying, now would you? In the case of a job interview, you would to prepare yourself for every possible scenario, every possible question, and of course, how you will respond to them. If you can, find out what types of job interviews the company typically conducts, and find out who will be giving the interview. Typically, companies use an interview process filled with multiple stages to weed out

applicants, which if this is the case, you'll want to be on top of your game each step of the way.

2) First you'll want to prepare for the types of job interview questions and answers.

Some will be standard questions that you should have a fairly easy time answering, such as, "Tell me a little bit about yourself," or, "What made you decide to get into this field?" The more difficult questions will follow, and will need much more thought to ensure you provide the interviewer with the appropriate answer while remaining true to yourself in the process.

Providing answers to tough interview questions can be difficult, but there is a way to handle it tactfully and gracefully. You must first assess yourself and determine your actual weaknesses, both personally and professionally. If you were let go from your previous job because you struggled with time management or couldn't complete projects on time, you'll have to figure out a way to address those without sounding incapable.

3) This goes along with number two - always try to turn a negative into a positive with job interview weakness questions. It sounds clichéd but it's true. Somehow you're going to have to make that lemon mentioned in number two into the best darn lemonade your potential employer ever tasted. Okay, maybe not to that extreme, but you need to

address it without sounding like you failed at your previous job.

If asked why you left your previous job, you could say, "There were some philosophical differences surrounding my department and our priorities as a group. Because of that, I didn't feel I was getting the support I needed to do my job to the best of my ability. Having a strong team surrounding me is very important." No need to get into details unless you're asked and no bluffing either. Craft your answer so you can have a chance at the job while keeping a clear conscience.

4) Research the company ahead of time. Familiarize yourself with the company's current projects, what direction it's heading in and of course, who's who. Then align your skills and experience up with it. This will come in handy when you're asked this deal-breaker, "Why do you think you'd be a good fit for our company?" By combining your skills and experience with the company, you're not only stating your capabilities, but creating a vision in their minds of what you can do for them.

5) Arrive promptly and prepared! Know where you'll be going ahead of time, and if possible, get directions and drive to the location of the interview prior to your interview time so you won't get lost. And however long you think it's going to take you to get there, assume it will take you 30 minutes

longer. Flat tires and dead car battery disasters have a funny way of sprouting up in the most inopportune moments.

Come prepared with questions of your own about the position and the company. This isn't just about what you can do for them. This is about what they can do for you as your potential employer. Bring a notepad to jot down notes and make sure to write down the names of who is giving you the interview on the notepad. Remembering names is a way of establishing rapport with people, and will go a long way in determining the success of your career. It's also important that you get the names of who interviewed you so that you can address the appropriate people when sending job interview thank you notes.

Guide to a Successful Job Interview

Are you ready for your next job interview? It's important to prepare properly to make an exceptional first impression on your interviewer.

✓ The day you start searching for a job:

- Make sure your cover letter and your resume have your complete contact details, such as your phone number and your email address.

- Don't have a long and silly voicemail greeting on your answering machine and or your cellular phone when expecting callbacks from interviewers.

- Most likely you will receive a short phone interview, before being invited to the office. Practice what you will say to catch interviewer's attention in 5-10 minutes.

✓ The day before the interview:

- Get a good night sleep. No need to worry the whole night.

- Print out the directions if you are not familiar with the area. Calculate the time needed for the road and add 30 minutes.

- Make sure that you know the name of the interviewer. Pronouncing it correctly will score you points.

- Don't get a haircut or buy a new outfit - if you are unhappy with the result it might bring some insecurity to the interview.

- Dress appropriately: men - wear a suit, women - knee length skirt or dress pants if you prefer, with a blouse, and be neat and professional. Don't use screaming bright colors, funky or latest fashion clothes, unless you are interviewing to be a fashion designer.

- Print out your resume and recommendation letters. Use good quality paper so that your resume will stand out from the rest. Print a second copy just in case there is a second interviewer present.

- Research the company you applying to - the Internet works well for this purpose. Find a few principles that stand out. Remember there is a good chance you'll be asked a few questions about the company: "What do you know about us?" and you don't want your answer to be: "Your building seems lovely!"

- Find the most common questions asked in an interview on the Internet and practice your answers in front of a mirror until there are no "umm", "yeah", "well, you know..." in your answers. You have to look confident and comfortable. But more importantly look natural and not rehearsed.

✓ The day of the interview:

- Dress for success and use a small amount of perfume/cologne - you don't want to give your interviewer a headache.

- It's better to be 15 minutes early that 1 minute late. If, for a very good reason you are still running late, make sure that you call the company and notify them of your situation.

- Have a breath mint while you are waiting.

- Turn off your cell phone and ensure that you remove your chewing gum.

- If presented with a job application, fill it out accurately and completely. Don't assume since you provide your resume that you don't need to fill that section out. Don't be lazy.

- Treat other people you meet with courtesy and respect. Trust me, people talk!

- Smile, greet, introduce yourself and offer a handshake when approaching the interviewer.

- Maintain good eye contact during the interview.

- Wait until you are offered to sit down. Don't slouch on the chair, don't rub your palms on your knees, don't touch/rub your nose, don't cross your arms, don't rub the back of your head or neck, don't use your pen as a drumstick, don't do anything that shows that you are nervous.

- Show enthusiasm about the position and the company.

- Don't give short "yes" and "no" answers, but at the same time don't tell your whole life story that will take a few hours. Your answers should be concise and informative.

- Don't interrupt your interviewer and don't try to make "smart" remarks to show that you know more on the subject than he does.

- Don't talk about your personal or financial issues .

- Don't complain about your previous boss or co-workers. Instead say that your schedule or proximity to work is not working out.

- Always remember that there will be a question that many of us wish we could avoid: "What are your weaknesses?". Use the weaknesses that do not matter for the job you applying for or that can be easily corrected. The most important thing is that you know your weaknesses and willing to work on them.

- An interview is not a one-sided conversation; instead, it is a mutual exchange of information. Remember to ask intelligent questions about the job, the company and the industry. Don't ever say you do not have any questions. Come up with something! You can always inquire about why the employee in this position left and what is expected from the new candidate.

- Don't inquire about the salary and benefits until after you've received an offer.

- Make sure that you understand the hiring process: know when and who would contact you next. Ask if there are any further steps you are expected to take.

- Try to get business cards from each person you interviewed with.

The day after the interview:

- A thank you email or a voicemail within 24 hours is mandatory but do not ask the status of your application or how did you do in the interview. Keep it brief as possible and do not seem over enthusiastic, as this can be perceived as being desperate and pushy.

Job interviews are scary, but they do not have to be with a good amount of practice and preparation.

Job Interviews - Tips For Identifying Your Strengths and Landing the Job You Want

All successful job interviews are based around a certain structure. This structure allows hiring managers to pick up on all of the main characteristics that will determine whether you are suitable for the position. One of the most predominant of these characteristics is your strengths.

Strengths are so broad that you can literally use any example, either in employment or personally outside of work. The great thing about talking about your strengths in an interview is that you can use non-work examples to cover up lack of experience or skills.

Ultimately, the employer is trying to ascertain whether you have the personality, attitude and capability to do the job in question. Therefore, skills can be learned but strengths are long term developments...meaning that if you don't have any strengths when applying for the job (in any capacity) then you're going to be far less desirable than your competitors.

Here's a few tips to identify your strengths when asked this potentially make or break question during an interview...

✓ Identifying Your Strengths

Start by asking friends and family what they would describe as your strengths as a person. Then ask your current employer for a more professional approach.

Finally, simply look over achievements you've made in your life and identify what strengths were required to make those particular achievements. This way, not only will you identify some of your best strengths (whether it be anything from positivity to typing skills...), but you will also have a clear example to give which will add much needed proof to your claims.

Let's look at some other strengths that you might want to consider...

✓ Strengths That Are Based On Work Skills

These are actual hands on strengths such as:

- Being able to type 60 words per minute,

- Being able to solve technical problems

- Being able to organize your daily tasks

- Being able to communicate effectively

✓ Emotional and mental strengths

Strengths can also be represented in your mental attitude. Some examples of this would be:

- Being able to handle stressful situations

- Being able to motivate yourself

- Being able to work well in a team

- Being able to cope with negativity and remain positive

- Being able to stay calm under pressure

Essentially, these are just a fraction of possible strengths you might posses. These types of strengths will always be welcomed with open arms in any job application. Providing you take the time to prepare some examples (which the employer might actually ask you for), then you stand a great chance of getting one step closer to winning that dream job.

Remember, every individual has their own strengths based on a unique combination of skills and mental attitude. Try to think beyond the obvious strengths you have, such as the example above, and think of key characteristics that people see in you above anyone else...

...because these are the strengths that will also set you apart in your job interview too.

How to Excel at Job Interview Preparation

There are many persons who need a job or want to change their current place of work, but simply cannot pass the interview stage. Even with a flawless resume and great credentials, it has become harder and harder for people to have a successful job interview and obtain the position they desire. With an increasingly larger number of companies and HR managers focusing on the social aspect of the work and on creating a perfect harmony in their corporate environment, there is a greater emphasis put on the personality and individual qualities of the person under scrutiny. Therefore, the large quantity of diplomas and years of experience in a field can simply fade away and make room for more modern requirements, such as multi-tasking abilities, group collaboration and leadership skills. The fact of the matter is that people need better job interview preparation if they want to succeed in gaining a certain highly requested position. The staff members in the recruiting departments are also getting better and better at determining the value of a potential employee in a split second, so why shouldn't you prepare as well? The work force is constantly changing and what was valuable a while ago is no longer important today. This being said, if you want to get inside the mind of the Human Resource representatives and other examiners you might encounter, here are some of the most useful tips for a job interview that will leave them speechless and convinced you are the one they are looking for.

The number one most important aspect of nailing a job interview lies in way you prepare for it in advance. This means research, years of studying the behaviour of specialists and analysing the way in which former employees were chosen, amongst many other aspects. It is a mountain of work and involves you have access to some confidential data, as well as corporate records. However, there is one method that can help you excel in getting a job opportunity faster and better. It evolves taking the advice of specialists in the field, especially those who have gone through the above mentioned steps and gathered all that precious information for you to have.

In addition to this, there is a high importance placed on how you act in front of the interviewers, whether or not you resemble his or her features and how to have the perfect timing and how much time you need to have in advance of the particular and many more particular details that you must know. You can call them the untold secrets of the recruiting world. The only way to excel in this endeavour and achieve the best job of your life is by training and being prepared.

Interview Preparation Tips - Amazing Techniques To Overcome Your Nerves

Most people are terrified when going to a job interview, If you are not prepared and feeling nervous, chances are you won't get hired. However if you are equipped with the right interview preparation tips, your goals and dream job can be yours. Here I will explain and teach you some handy interview preparation tips that you never thought possible.

1. Punctuality - when you go to a job interview it's always good to show up on time but I suggest show up at least 15-10 minutes earlier, as it shows the employer that you are very good at punctuality, and it prevents the employer from asking you about your punctuality with previous employers. When your in an interview try and mention that you show up to work everyday and on time, the last thing any employer wants is someone that isn't going to show up to work when they're suppose to.

2. Body Language - most people seem to forget this one but it's human nature, our bodies can tell stories without us knowing it, especially employers they have a keen eye for body language, sit with a good posture and make as much eye contact as possible, less eye contact means you are not interested in what the employer is saying, prospective employers wouldn't want to work with some one that doesn't have an interest in the job position, also always put

your shoulders back it tells your employer that you are confident even if you did not say it, when you are confident you can complete any task assigned to you.

3. Talking About Yourself - this is where you sell yourself, you make the most of your opportunities here to mention all the good qualities and benefits you will bring to the company, Using these interview preparation tips will get you a lot more success to gaining the job you want, some people sell themselves short by simply forgetting the basics of a job interview. Talking about yourself and adding value to your application is the best way to get hired.

Once you get hired from a company always keep up with your commitments and attend work every day, if you intend of being absent be sure to contact your employer, it can be a recipe to get sacked if anyone fails to keep up with their punctuality, not only can you use your body language at an interview to have a positive outcome but you can also use it once you're hired, always have a good posture to show your confident at work, When your at an interview remember to talk about yourself once you get the chance and by all means sell yourself as much as you can and highlight all your benefits backed up with experience.

How to Prepare For a Behavioral Interview

What is a behavioral interview? The primary focus of behavioral interviewing is not on whether you can do this or that task in the future, that is, with this organization, but have you done this or that task in the past and given your experience how effectively you can communicate what you have done to the interviewer. You are expected to give specific examples. As a result, you need to describe a particular event or project or experience describing how you dealt with the situation and what the result of outcome of that experience was.

The Response Model. As the candidate, your response to questions need to be specific and detailed. Listen to the question. Clarify any points that are unclear to you then frame your responses in a structured way. For example,

Briefly, identify a particular situation that relates to the question;

Identify what you did specifically in that situation; and

Identify what the result or outcome was (hopefully, there was a positive result). You can layer your responses. Think of an onion. The outer layers provide the other person with the big picture or the bottom line of your proposal. Each subsequent layer reveals more and more detail.

The Art Part. The interviewer asks you a question. You respond. If the interview process is "canned," the interviewer will go on to the next question. If the interviewer is focused on how you responded, (s)he could pick up on one or two points in your response to get more detail. For example, the interviewer may ask you, "What was going through your mind at that point?" Or, "Tell me more about how you handled that person." Or, "Walk me through your decision making process." Or, "Why did you decide to do what you did?" Or, "How did your customer/team/direct reports react when you did that?" If you are asked a hypothetical question, such as "What if..." or "What would you do if..." acknowledge this as a hypothetical question and respond accordingly.

It is not necessary to build a watch when responding. Respond to the question as succinctly and directly as you can. It is not necessary to fill the air with your voice. When interviewers want more detail, they will ask you another question that gets at that detail.

Some interviewers want to create stress. They want to see how you handle that stress. Interviewers can create a little fun for themselves by asking you multiple questions at the same time. There may be two interviewers in the room. Each could ask you a question at the same time. Do not panic. Listen to each question. Select one (the easier of the two) to answer first. Then ask the other interviewer to repeat his or her other question. If the questions were designed to cause you stress, the interviewer may dismiss the question and move on or ask you an entirely different question. If the questions were not designed to cause you stress, chances are the interviewer will repeat the question and allow you to answer it.

Preparation before you Talk. Traditional interviews include items such as "Tell me about yourself." "What are your greatest strengths and weaknesses?" "Why do you want to work for us?" "Where do you see yourself in five years?" Often, the person doing the interviewing does more talking than the person being interviewed. You may think this is a good idea, but be careful. You are one of perhaps dozens of people applying for this position. You need to create a clear picture of your strengths for this interviewer. Typically the interviewer has a set of questions for specific competency areas, such as communication, decision making, planning, team building, managing others, and so on. As a starting point, prepare specific responses for these types questions.

Give me an example of when you had to make a quick decision.

Describe an example of an important goal you had to set and how you reached that goal.

Describe a situation where you had to deal with a very complex set of issues and how you resolved them.

How do you establish performance expectations with an employee (if this a managerial position)?

How have you confronted an employee who did not perform up to your expectations?

What are your basic values and beliefs when you delegate something to someone?

Tell me about an experience where you had to present an opposing viewpoint. How did you get your point across? What was the outcome?

Tell me about a time when a client (internal or external) requested that you take an approach or implement a solution that you did not agree with. What was the situation? Why didn't you agree with it? How did you handle it? What was the outcome?

What in your experience makes you believe that you would be a good fit for this position, department?

Make certain you are honest with yourself. What are your weaknesses? Why are they weaknesses? And how would you respond if someone asked you if you had any of these problems or traits?

- Procrastination
- Tardiness or Family related issues
- Problems working with people who are different than you

- Preference for working alone (or working in a group)
- Difficulties dealing with authority figures
- Difficulties dealing with poor performers
- Difficulties dealing with conflict

Your self-image and self-esteem

You could say that you have no weaknesses, or at least not those weaknesses. If you choose that route, be prepared to identify at least one thing that is not high on your strength list. We all have weaknesses and by identifying one you are in a better position to control this part of the interview. And do not forget to have your own set of questions to ask the interviewer. Consider these sample questions to ask the interviewer as you move through the interview.

Can you tell me something about the manager of this department, e.g., his or her style of leadership, what (s)he expects from people?

What is the turnover of personnel in this department?

Why is there an opening in this department at this time?

How would you describe someone from that department who is very successful?

What is the most stressful or difficult or demanding part of this job?

Telephone Job Interviews - Win with Preparation

As recently as 15 years ago the phone interview was used rarely in the recruitment process. Today company recruiters use the phone interview as an essential tool in winnowing the list of qualified candidates to a short list of candidates to be invited in for a face-to-face interview.

The phone interview should be approached differently from the face-to-face meeting as what you say and how you say it will become vital in moving to the next level. Keep that in mind as you prepare for winning the phone interview. Here are some tips to help in your preparation:

1. Focus on the phone interview. Get rid of all the distractions. Turn off the cell phone and computer. If you get a call for the phone interview and the time is not convenient, reschedule it for a better time.

Treat the phone interview as if you were looking the person on the other end of the line directly in the eye. Pay attention as if the person were in the room with you. Smile when you talk and be sure there is energy in your voice. If necessary practice the interview with a friend. Tape and critique the conversation. Do it until you get it right and you are comfortable with your performance. An interesting tip:

Remain standing during the telephone interview. Normally this will give you more energy in your voice.

2. Clearness counts. Keep from rambling. Stick to the point. Make sure you have properly heard and understand the question. If unclear ask for clarification.

What are the two or three critical skills required for the position? In your interview preparation put together a short powerful response directly addressing each required skill. Weave these answers into the conversation. It might be a short story illustrating your ability or reference to your proficiency to achieve planned results.

3. Overall preparation is the key. Since the telephone interview is designed to screen you out you must make every attempt to connect with the interviewer. On way to do this is to prepare in advance what questions you might ask when prompted by the interviewer.

You do not want the telephone interview to be conducted so you spend the entire time simply answering questions. If so you will miss opportunities to deliver key points relative to how you skills match what is required by the employer. Prepare examples, stories and anecdotes that back up how your skills and abilities would be a good fit for the position.

Your goal should be to be personable, friendly and be able to relate to the interviewer. For example, questions you might ask include: What are the one or two top challenges in the position? Carefully listen to the answer and then respond with a short example where you faced similar challenges at another position and achieved excellent results. You should have a list of 3 to 7 questions of this nature with short responses to the answer received that reflect favorably on your abilities and strengths.

With this preparation for the phone interview you should sail through to the next level. Build on what you learned in the phone interview to prepare for a winning face-to-face interview.

Behavioural Interview Technique - Guarantee Success With 5 Simple Tips

Behavioral interview technique is becoming more important because "Behavioral" job interviews are becoming more and more common, and may eventually replace the "standard" style of interviewing. The basic premise of this kind of interview is the assumption that your behavior in the past is an accurate indicator of how you will behave in future. If your behavioral interview technique needs some work, check out these quick tips.

✓ Visualize the questions-

Before you go into the interview, spend some time imagining what kinds of questions you are going to be asked. Make a brief list of them, and then using the list try and imagine why they are asking each question. This is a great behavioral interview technique, and will give you a head start for the next tip...

✓ Visualize the answers-

Spend some time thinking over your working career, and problems you may have solved or helped solve, or situations you may have been able to improve. Questions related to such things will likely come up, so it's a good idea to have a few examples ready to give.

✓ Exaggerate-

Well, kind of. Always remember that the examples you give are completely up to you-if your own life experiences don't match up EXACTLY to what they are asking of you, you may well have to "bend" it a little, to encompass the skills and experience they want to know about. Bear in mind that every other candidate will be doing this also, so you may need to to keep your behavioral interview technique up to scratch!

✓ Be prepared to expand-

An employer will rarely just take your first answer and move on; more likely they will want to delve a little deeper and get into further detail. If you are prepared for this you can make your answers very convincing. If you can also somehow relate your answers to the things you raised with the first tip (visualizing questions), this can be a very powerful technique for behavioral job interviews, and can bring lots of success.

✓ Don't limit yourself-

The past experiences they ask about need not be work related-If you play for a recreational sports team or you have other "outside" activities, they can all potentially be used as examples for you. This is a very useful behavioral interview technique for people who may have recently graduated or recently entered the job market for other reasons-college/school projects and examples of your behavior can be just as valid as examples given from the workplace.

The behavioral interview is not necessarily as difficult a technique to master as people first assume, it just requires some careful though beforehand!

How to Win Your Ideal Role (job)- CV and Interview Preparation

Looking for jobs can be stressful. The process can be long, and landing your ideal job requires you to perform well every step of the way. The best way to handle the daunting task of landing a new role is to focus on each step as it comes. This step-by-step guide will offer tips on how to prep your CV, write a winning cover letter, and perform your best at the inevitable interview.

✓ How to prep your CV

The sole purpose of your CV is to catch the attention of your potential employer in order to get you an interview. A CV isn't meant to display your design skills, but to act as your own personal marketing tool. Writing punchy headlines and keeping the design simple and clear will catch the reader's attention and urge them to read on.

The most important thing about your resume is that the content is engaging and paints you in a true, positive light. Instead of listing your responsibilities, include how your skills and experience helped your employer. Always include a list of your successes, and if possible, use numbers to back up those successes.

When writing your CV, remember who your reader is. Identify what they will be looking for, and make sure you know the skills needed for the role you're applying for. If you do your homework on the company and its employees, you will be able to better understand how to present your skills and experiences to them. It will help you decide if the business meets your needs, and if you meet theirs.

✓ Write a great cover letter

While your CV is the main event, your cover letter is what will entice an employer to read it. The intended function of the cover letter is to outline the relevant parts of your CV.

Here are some pointers on how to best write your letter:

1. Find out who your letter should be addressed to, either by calling the company and asking, or doing research on LinkedIn or the company website. If you can't find the right person, write to a senior member of staff, who will hopefully pass it on to the right person. If they pass it on with a request to contact you, then the chances of the person in charge of hiring not calling you back are slim - who's going to ignore a request from the boss?

2. Ignore your instincts and axe the formal tone. Being yourself will allow recruiters to assess whether you're suited for the role

3. Try a bold approach: state a time when you will follow up with them, and then make sure you do.

4. If you're submitting your application in hard copy, hand-write the recipient's name and address. Most people open handwritten mail first.

5. If you're submitting an application via email, craft an interesting subject line. For example, you could use: "Introduction from... " and then explain why that person gave you their email address.

6. Try to answer these questions: "What do they want to know" and "How am I going to add value to the team?" Let the answers to these questions guide your writing.

7. Tell them why you want to work for their company and why you want the position.

✓ Perform well at interview

You've made it to the most important stage, thanks to your cover letter and CV. While interviews are often nerve-racking and can make the calmest of people nervous, there are things that you can do to decrease your anxiety.

The way that you present yourself is important in an interview. Always dress up, and make sure that you shake hands firmly, make eye contact, and are happy and excited about the job opportunity.

Remember that preparation is key. Make sure you know where you're going and have a copy of your CV on hand. It is also important to research the company you're interviewing with in case they ask the question: "What do you know about our company?" The research you do will also allow you to formulate questions to ask at the end of your interview, and to assess whether this is the ideal company for you.

In face-to-face interviews, many employers ask competency-based questions as a way for you to prove that you're competent and suited for the job through your past experience. Never lie, be yourself, and don't use the same example twice.

By preparing and believing in yourself, you're going into an interview with the right attitude. All the work you've put into your CV and cover letter have paid off, and remember that you wouldn't be at the interview stage if you weren't qualified.

Chapter 2 : How to Perfectly answer Interview Questions!

The Importance of Understanding Job Interview Questions

If you're trying to figure out how to ace a job interview, then you better start taking some notes. More important than your resume or the outfit you wear; your answers to interview questions will lead you to success. The key to brilliant answers is understanding the questions.

You need to clearly understand the question at hand and think about your answer before speaking. If you do not know what the interviewer is looking for, you will not be able to produce a worthy answer.

The interviewers can ask a range of questions. These questions can range from your personality and behavior, to past job experience and education. Every question they ask has a purpose, sometimes even beyond what they're asking. Some interviewers ask their questions to gauge how you'll respond to certain situations and certain pressures. However, they mainly want to know more about you and your experiences - the overall point of an interview is never to simply put the candidate on the spot.

You should do a variety of research before you walk into an interview. It is important to figure out what are the commonly asked questions. Once you know about the different types of questions, you will be able to think of responses that are relevant, so that you can tell your interviewer exactly what they want to know about you.

How to Answer Job Interview Questions - A Quick Reference Guide

Going for an interview is never easy, you feel nervous and ill at ease. And then, of course, are the questions that come shooting at you from the interviewer, questions which you think you shall not be able to handle. But with beforehand preparation, you can know how to answer job interview questions.

When it comes to knowing how to answer job interview questions, there will usually be that first question - "Why don't you tell me about yourself?" Well, basically the interviewer is looking for a brief biography of yours, but you have to be careful not to ramble on.

He won't want to hear about your high school prom! Tell your interview relevant details to the job, for example - if you have worked at some other job that is related to this one. Communicate what you have to say clearly and effectively.

Always remember to...

Sometimes interviewers also ask why you left your last job. It's important to know how to answer job interview questions, and here you should carefully refrain from being negative about your last employers - it only sheds bad light on you.

Tell the truth - if you were let go, say so, but don't dwell on it, stress that you want to make a fresh start.

Since we are telling you how to answer job interview questions, you should also know how to answer "What do you expect from us?"

Be as concise as possible, avoid going into details and sounding overly confident at this point. Instead, it would be a good idea to say that you hope the company can help you achieve your goals, and that you, in turn, would love to do a lot for the company.

If you know how to answer job interview questions, it makes things a lot easier, and in this article, we have shown you simple ways how to answer job interview questions.

Most Common Interview Questions and How to Answer Them

Any job seeker must have noticed the most common interview questions and wonder how to answer them. When a person is invited for a job interview, there will be some questions from other previous job interviews that are likely to be repeated. These questions are general questions commonly asked about your personal background and how you work in the office. Answering these common questions with honest and well thought-out answers will help you get the job.

The following list of most common interview questions and how to answer them will surely help you prepare for any job interviews in the future. Here are the most common interview questions and how to answer them correctly:

1.) Tell me about yourself.

This has to be the most universal question of all time. It would be rare for a job interview not to start with this question. It is very tricky because the question encompasses all the things about you. The secret to answering this question is focusing on information that you can use for the job you are applying for.

The interviewer does not want you to tell him about your life story, just focus on the vital details about you and your job experiences. Give a little background on your education (citing a few awards, honors and scholarships), then on your previous employments (mention your duties and responsibilities), and your current situation.

You can also add a few of your long and short term goals. But avoid mentioning any plan to change your career in a few years time.

2.) Describe yourself.

This is your chance to present yourself in the best way possible without sounding arrogant or cocky. Avoid using adjectives to describe yourself. For instance, instead of saying, "I am very focused." you can say, "I am the type of person who pays attention to details."

3.) What do your co-workers say about you?

You need to give a specific quote or paraphrase of a boss' or a co-worker's observation about you. You can say, "When I gave my resignation letter to my boss, he asked me to reconsider my resignation because he feels that I can get the job done on time and he really likes how I handle the tasks diligently." Or you can say, "My coworkers often mention that they like how I'm always enthusiastic." Mentioning such statements would be as good as your boss or co-workers telling those great things about you. Again avoid using adjectives such as "My coworkers describe me as friendly."

4.) Why did you leave your last job?

No matter what your reason for leaving your previous job, never put your former employer in a bad light. Never bad mouth your previous boss even if you resigned because of his negative attitude. Avoid mentioning the huge salary if this was what attracted you to the job. The best way to answer this question is by telling the interviewer that you are seeking a career advancement or a better job opportunity.

5.) Why should we hire you?

Answer this by mentioning your qualifications. Use your resume as your guide but avoid reading it. The important thing is for the interviewer to see that you are an asset to the company. Avoid mentioning any benefits that you can get from the job, but rather focus on WHY THE COMPANY NEEDS YOU.

6.) What experience do you have in this field?

Answer with specific experience or previous tasks that you were part of in your previous job that relates to the position or the field. If you do not have enough experience, try to mention job experiences that are nearest to the job.

7.) What's your biggest strength/weakness?

It is easy to answer your biggest strength. Just mention what you are good at and you're okay.

The problem now is your weakness. Avoid answering this too honestly, or you might ruin your chances. Also, never give a fake answer like, "I'm too committed to the job." Say a negative thing about you in the past and MENTION HOW YOU OVERCAME IT. For instance you may say, "I had a problem with organizing, so I decided to use an organizer and a small notebook to create check lists of my daily and weekly tasks. I follow the schedules religiously."

8.) Are you a team player?

Yes! You are a team player. Cite examples of how you are a team player. Mention projects that you were a part of that have been successful.

9.) How do you work under pressure?

Answer this positively. Mention a few examples when working under pressure. Make it seem as though working under pressure was the norm in your previous job. Avoid saying that you panic or crumble when under pressure.

10.) What kind of salary do you expect?

Never answer with a number. Tell the interviewer that you are willing to consider what the company can offer.

Behavioral Interview Questions and Answers - Tips and Advice

Behavioral interviews are becoming more and more popular in this highly competitive job market. The main reason that employers like the behavioral interview is that it can predict the future actions of candidates quite accurately. What do we mean by this?

Traditional interview questions - the ones you may be more used to - typically call for highly objective answers and can be based on misperceptions. For instance, how you answer the question, "What are your strengths and weaknesses?" is based on your own perception of yourself. Since the employer does not yet know you, he or she cannot judge the accuracy of your answers.

However, behavioral interview questions provide the interviewer with much greater insight into how your mind works. As the name implies, behavioral questions focus on just that: your actual behavior - and not your perceptions. In this type of interview, the interviewer has targeted several specific behaviors and attitudes that the job requires, and has designed behavioral interview questions that will shed light on whether you might be a good fit for the position.

✓ Behavioral questions examples

Here are some typical interview behavioral questions:

*Tell me about a time when you had to make a decision without sufficient information. How did the situation work out?

*Tell me about a time when you had to work with someone who did not like you. How did you deal with the situation? What was the outcome?

*Describe a decision you made that was unpopular. Why did you make the decision? How did you sell your decision? What was the outcome?

*If you are given an assignment that you don't know how to handle, what would you do?

*What would you do if a customer complains about you to your boss?

*Tell me about a time when someone's interruptions were in danger of causing you to miss a deadline. What did you do?

Notice how much more specific and detailed this type of question is than traditional, straightforward interview questions. The idea behind the success of behavioral questions & answers is that a person's past performance is a good indicator of his or her future performance.

✓ Navigating behavioral questions & answers

While answering this type of question may seem more difficult than traditional questions, actually, with a little practice, you may find that the answers come more naturally since you're simply recalling your past experiences. Here are some guidelines to keep in mind for answering behavioral questions in a way that will help your interviewer the most:

*Always relate the question to a specific instance in your career.

*Describe the tasks that were related to the instance. What was the expected outcome?

*Describe your actions in relation to the task or instance. What did you do? Why did you decide to do it?

*Always describe the actual outcome of your actions, even if it wasn't favorable. What did you learn from the experience? What might you do differently if faced with a similar situation?

In answering interview behavioral questions this thoroughly, you show that you understand what the interviewer is looking for and that you're willing to offer up the information to help them make the best decision.

✓ Additional tips

*Remember, there are no right or wrong answers. Just answer the question as honestly as you can, while focusing on describing your actions during the situation.

*Don't feel attacked by the interviewer's follow up questions, which may feel very probing. The interviewer is simply trying to understand how and why you've acted in situations he or she believes related to the job, and is not personally attacking you.

*Relax and take a deep breath before answering. It's OK to take a few minutes to think of your answer.

*If you're describing a stressful situation, avoid the temptation to get upset all over again. Detach yourself from the emotions of the situation, and describe the details as factually as possible.

*Smile! Speak smoothly and confidently.

With some practice and preparation, you'll find that you can handle the more difficult behavioral interview questions successfully and with confidence.

Answers to Interview Questions - The Best Reference Guide

The very thought of an interview can freak some people out, especially if there answers to interview questions do anything but impress the interviewers.

Preparing thoroughly for expected questions and preparing the right answers to interview questions is how you can succeed in a job interview.

The following should give you some idea about the appropriate answers to questions that you are most likely to encounter.

Q: Introduce yourself.

When the interviewers ask the questions that involve your introduction, they are not interested in your personal details or a biographical account in your answers. Carefully construct answers to such interview questions, which briefly describe your career to the interviewer highlighting your achievements and skills.

Q: What are your goals and aspirations?

Don't get carried away as you deliver your answers to this type of interview questions, and don't start elaborating your extensive list of personal to-do list. Instead focus on your professional abilities, while explaining how they can be beneficial to your employer in your answers to such questions.

Q: Why do you want this job?

This is one of the most commonly asked questions in a job interview. Such interview questions are a good opportunity for you to give answers that separate you from the rest of the candidates. In fact, through these kinds of interview questions, the interviewers judge whether you are the right person for the job by your answers. The best way to deal with such interview questions is to mention your skills and experience to be crucial in adding value to the business of your employer in your answers. Your answers to such interview questions should primarily be addressing the needs of the employer.

Q: What are your strengths?

Prepare your answers to such questions carefully by listing down your best skills that you have learned with experience, so you are able to convey them to the interviewer with confidence and ease in your answers to this interview question.

Q: What are your weaknesses?

While being careful that you do not mention something really serious in your answers to such questions, you can identify an area of weakness in your professional abilities, which could be like difficulty in speaking publicly. But as you mention your weaknesses in your answers to such interview questions, they should be accompanied by the steps that you are taking to make improvements in them.

Q: Why did you leave your last job?

Since such questions could involve a discussion about your previous employer, be very careful that you don't start an attack on your previous employer in your answers to them. Do not present your interviewer with a list of reasons why the last job was not right for you in your answers to such interview questions.

Be careful to maintain a positive approach towards answering every question. You should instead answer this question by explaining your professional aspirations, and that although your previous job was a decent one, joining the new organization could help the growth of a particular dimension of your career, for example, creativity. Support your answers to such questions by talking about what you have learned previously and how you could use that in the new position.

Ten Most Common Interview Questions

Being a qualified candidate for any job cannot be measured only by your educational attainment. One has to be adept in establishing good impressions. And to be able to stand out among other applicants, get ready ahead of time through knowing the most common interview questions so as to be able to give the best answers. A typical interview will probably consist of the following interview questions and answers:

1. Among all the inquiries, being asked to tell about yourself is the top choice for any employer. Others will claim they are hardworking, loyal and dependable. Remember that you have to be remarkable while not appearing nonchalant or arrogant. Introduce yourself with the use of the Unique Selling Proposition which is a factual brief sentence. This has been used for many years by numerous brand labels. This is effective to generate the recall factor. For example, "I have been an active researcher of (company name) for 3 years now, wherein I spearheaded several fact-finding missions and module drafting under the urban community development program." The conversation will then turn to your favor as you already established different points of interest for your work history.

2. Now that you are selling yourself, be careful in answering the query "why should we hire you". Expand on your

achievements, abilities, knowledge and skills. Note that everything you will say has to be correlated to the position in order to make the interviewer see you can be an "asset to this organization." A portfolio of your output can substantiate your claims.

3. When you are asked, "What is your greatest weakness?" do not hesitate to be honest. Sometimes accepting defeat will show people how you balance your professional life. Tell him that through recognizing your flaw, you have developed ways to improve your skills and manner of responding to a particular situation. This then can also become your greatest strength, which is to have foresight and open-mindedness.

4. Another eminent question regards "what work environment do you prefer?" The interviewer will ask this leading question so as he can have an overview whether you are a team player or otherwise. It would be safe to answer that you have worked efficiently both in team efforts or individual tasks.

5. If you are asked how you handle stress, keep in mind to project a positive attitude towards this situation. Just describe how you respond to problems such as taking a breather, practicing meditation exercises or immediately devising solutions rather than delving into depression.

6. "Why did you leave your last job?" is perhaps one of the most intriguing questions. First of all, do not speak negatively of your previous work. Tell him that you left

because you want growth in learning new things and experiencing a new environment. However, disclose any legal issues or pertinent problems as this company will probably ask your former employer for an evaluation.

7. Conversely, if you have been unemployed for a few months now, the interviewer will inquire, "What were you busy about since your last job?" Say that you have been working on improving your craft or had to attend personal matters like death or illness. Once again, such claims should be validated through certificates or other documentation files.

8. Towards the end of the interview, you will be asked, "how much salary do you need?" Do over/underestimate your and the company's worth. Research beforehand about the salary per employee level the organization offers. Evaluate your skills, experience and knowledge and analyze as to which tier you belong to. Then you can safely say that you found out this specific amount is the compensation for an employee in their company range.

9. You may also be asked why you want to work for their company. Tell him that you have given in-depth thoughts why you firstly applied for the position. Say that the goals and interests of the company are parallel to the things you are passionate about. Make your past experiences come into play so as to prove this particular position in the line of your field.

10. Lastly, you will also be tested as how long you will see yourself working for them. When you are asked how do you see yourself in five years or so, simply say that a part of your long-term goals is to thrive financially and professionally. And you can only do that with their company.

All these questions are a test of your strength of character and sincerity. Thus, it is important that you must truly believe in everything you will say so as to manifest how seriously want to get the job.

Lifeguard Interview Question and Answer Tips

Congratulations on becoming the newest lifesaving, action taking, challenge meeting professional lifeguard by completing your lifeguard certification exams! Now, it's time to move forward and take those new skills and that deep driven passion to help others and find your first lifeguard job.

Although it takes a special kind of candidate to fit the role and demands of a lifeguard, many of the most common lifeguard interview questions are based on common sense and to test your ambition to simply ensure that you have what it takes to make the team. Much like any career or job, the interview is a chance for both the candidate and the potential employer to get a feel for each other and see how compatible the relationship may be before moving forward.

Before you set off to take on the interview questions head on, here is a list of some of the most common lifeguard interview questions that you may want to prepare yourself for. Take these questions seriously, but do not feel threatened or anxious, as they are merely tools in making sure you can provide the right fit for the job.

Please feel free to tell us a little bit about yourself and about your lifeguard certification and training.

Obviously, the relationship between employer and employee needs to be healthy and compatible, so be open and share yourself as an individual. Be upfront and proud of your training and your lifeguard certification credentials as these are important for your interviewer to know all about.

Why do you feel that you would make a good fit in our team as a lifeguard?

This is your chance to 'sell yourself' and show your potential employer why they should consider you for the position. Don't hold back, but don't get cocky, either!

In your own opinion, what is the definition of "integrity" and how does it apply to the position you are seeking?

Professionalism, maturity and reliability are key points to make in order for you to present yourself as a valuable asset. The responsibilities of a lifeguard are heavy and this is an opportunity to show your potential employer that you have what it takes to spearhead the challenges.

What do you believe are qualities that make for a successful aquatic program?

Show a firm belief in the facilities mission and vision in providing customer service and ensuring that the facilities patrons and customer are safe. Prior to the interview, do some research on the facility and find the information before you ever step foot into the interview.

How would you plan on enforcing rules and regulations of the facility and the program?

This is a chance to show off your customer service skills, yet also to show that you can be firm and provide the "show of strength" in being able to respect the facility regulations.

How would you manage difficult customers?

There are some basic skills here, but the most important one is to - LISTEN - to the customer. In many cases, customers become unruly because they feel that they are not being listened to. Empathize with the difficult customer and let them feel understood, then deal with the issue as professionally and mutually beneficial as possible.

Describe some important qualities to have when working with children.

Children LOVE playing in the water - unfortunately, many young children are not experienced swimmers and lifeguards must take extra caution in ensuring that both parents and children are properly monitored. Children scare easily, so emergency situations can bring some unique challenges when children are involved.

What do you believe are the most important characteristics of a lifeguard?

Illustrate the importance of what you learned in your lifeguard certification program and training.

Professionalism, maturity, reliability and maintaining a positive attitude are just a few.

What are you looking to gain from your employment here if you were hired?

Share your planned career path and don't be afraid to ask questions, but it is good to have a structured plan on where you see yourself as a professional lifeguard later on as well.

Why should we consider you for this position?

More than likely, you are competing with other candidates for the position you are interviewing for. This is possibly a second opportunity to sell yourself and push your name ahead of the list. Be honest and again, show your passion and desire for why you applied for the position in the first place.

Common sense and honesty are two of the most important factors that you can bring to the interview that can help you get the job you're looking for. Your hard work and dedication to get your lifeguard certification credentials can be used in showing your potential employer how ambitious you are in becoming a rescue service professional and move forward in your career as a lifeguard.

Good luck!

How to Handle Difficult Interview Questions

You are in the middle of an important interview and are confident that you are doing an excellent job of presenting your skills and qualifications for the position. The interviewer asks the next question - and it's a difficult one. You didn't see this question coming and have no idea to answer it. Words catch in your mouth. You start to sweat as your illustrious visions of landing your dream job are rapidly spiraling away at a breakneck speed. What do you do?

For starters, the best offense is a good defense. Preparing for an interview in advance is the best way to ensure that you will be at your peak performance when the time comes to answer the question "Why should you get this job?". Compile a list of interview questions, both general questions and those that are job-specific, that you could potentially be asked. Then practice answering all of the questions. It may be necessary to practice some questions several times until you can clearly present a solid answer. A good rule of thumb is to practice until you are no longer uncomfortable with the question itself or your resulting answer.

Tempting as it may be to dismiss more straightforward questions, such as "Tell me about yourself", you should rehearse your answer to every question. Oftentimes job applicants get so caught up in preparing for the "tough" questions, that they neglect the ones they perceive to be the "easier" ones. As a result, they are ill-prepared to answer basic questions and stumble in their answers.

It would be impossible to think of and practice every question you could be asked, so you will inevitably run across some questions during the interview process that you hadn't thought of previously. When this happens, the first thing to do is take a deep breath. Repeat the question to yourself, either in your head or aloud to the interviewer, to ensure that you have heard the question correctly. Then use your practice sessions to draw correlations between this question and others you have practiced. Is this new question a variation of one you have answered before? Is it similar to any other question? If you can draw a parallel to questions you are already comfortable with, then the new question will not appear so daunting.

Another good tactic is to break the question into smaller components so that you can take it bit by bit. This is especially useful for multi-part questions. For example, imagine you are asked: "Tell me about a time when you found yourself at odds with a team member. What were the circumstances and how did you handle the confrontation". The first thing to do is break this into two parts: (1) provide an example of a team member confrontation, and (2) how did the confrontation get resolved. When answering this question, focus entirely on the first part initially. Set the stage for the conflict that arose, giving the interviewer all of the necessary details. Once this is done, you can then move onto the next part, which is detailing how the conflict was resolved. This is truly the "meat" of the question. The interviewer is more interested in hearing about how you handle conflict and stressful situations than the actual specifics of the conflict itself. So don't skimp on the second part - the resolution. This pattern is true of a majority of multi-part questions: one section of the answer is merely the opportunity to set the stage for the other, more pertinent part(s) of the question.

If you are asked a question you don't know the answer to, it is often better to admit that are unsure of the answer than to try and buffalo your way though an answer. Most interviewers are highly experienced at recognizing "BS" answers and can easily pick up that you making stuff up. If this happens, they will either call you on the table about your fake answer or write you off a being a fraud - neither of these is going to help you land a job. An appropriate response would be to admit that you do not have an answer for the question, but that you would like to do some research at the conclusion of the interview so that you have this knowledge for future reference. Such an answer not only shows integrity, but it also shows that you are not adverse to expanding your learning and are willing to take the extra effort necessary to keep your skills sharp.

A few other helpful hints for answering difficult questions:

It is okay to ask the interviewer to repeat the question if you didn't hear it the first time or if it is a long multi-part question.

It is also okay to ask the interviewer for clarification if the question is unclear.

Never volunteer personal information that is not job-related.

Try to always turn negatives into positives. For example, when asked about your weaknesses, demonstrate how this weakness can also be an asset in other areas.

Relax! Interviewing is a learning process and you will get stronger each time you interview for a potential position. So if an interview goes bad, rather than dwell on it, identify where things went wrong and work on correcting those areas so that you can perform better in your next interview.

When I Didn't Know the Answer to an Interview Question! (7 Expert Tips to Handle Such Situation)

Can there be a better way of handling the situation, when a candidate does not have an answer to a question asked during interview?

Now, there may not be an infallible strategy to encounter such a situation, but I can suggest a few ways which can act as a graceful mechanism to manage such disaster. However, it would be wiser if we start by identifying the situations that may arise and devise the strategies apropos to the respective situations. Following are the instances in which a candidate may be dumb-founded:

- When the interviewee didn't understand the meaning of a question or a word - Strong communication skills, and an ability to comprehend the conversation are among the greatest demands of current business environment. Emphatically, a candidate must possess strong communication skills that include a strong vocabulary too so that one doesn't stagger at any question asked by interviewer. However, no person in this world may attain an exhaustive vocabulary. A situation may still arise as it happened with one of the candidates, when interviewer asked, "What are your pet peeves?" Unfortunately, the candidate, though well spoken, didn't know the meaning of the word 'peeves'. But did the candidate panic? No! Or did she say, "sorry, but I don't know the meaning of that word, or 'I didn't understand the question', or 'I don't know the answer'." Candidate could have said any of the above, but she did not. Instead, she politely requested, "Could you please rephrase the question?" Implication is the same, but it was an extremely positive way of saying the same thing. An interviewer deals with several candidates daily, and is aware that candidates are not expected to know every word. Interviewer is trying to find out if you have the ability to choose positive or smart words to say the same thing. Having said that, it's imperative to build strong language skills, because you can't ask an interviewer to rephrase every question. However, for an instance or two, use the strategy discussed above. First advice: "Request the recruiter, choosing a positive set of words, to rephrase the question."

- When a question asked was out of a topic that was never covered in your curriculum or was not a part of your job profile - Ideally, a recruiter would never ask you about something unless he doesn't expect you to have learned or experienced it as a part of your education or work profile. But, what can you possibly do in a situation, when you never did or studied what recruiter asked about? You could've simply told the recruiter that you never did what he was asking for, and interviewer should stick to what's mentioned in the resume. But wait! Let's rephrase the same thing to your maximum advantage. You could simply present the same thing in much stronger way by saying, "During my education and experience, I have garnered strong technical know-how and expertise. I can understand that the skill that you mentioned must be of great importance to this role, and I would love to learn that new skill through training and guidance. I am sure that my existing knowledge combined with this new skill will enable me to deliver a performance beyond expectations. However, I would like to know from you the importance of this skill in this role" Through this answer, you stressed on your current capabilities, because of which you were invited for this interview; you also showed your openness towards developing new skills; you gave recruiter a thought that this skill could simply be learned through training and guidance; finally, you made recruiter re-think whether this skill was actually required in this role or not. Most importantly, you told the recruiter that you didn't know it without actually saying it. But you can't keep answering 'I will learn' to every question asked. It is strictly for something out of the blue. Second advice: "Never say you don't know it. Say you can learn it."

- When, in a behavioral question, you actually had never faced the situation given by recruiter - One thing must always be kept in mind that recruiter is highly aware of what he or she is asking for. Your answer to a situational or behavioral question demonstrates your ability to cope with the pressure of working in teams, and dealing with a large pool of people with various mind sets, especially in case of large cross-functional teams. So how would you tell your interviewer that you had never faced a disagreement with another team member, or supervisor, or the management? Actually, you don't! Never say that you don't have an idea because you never came across such a situation for any of the situational or behavioral questions. However, you can start by saying, "Apologies for not being able to share a real experience since it hasn't happened yet, but if such a situation comes, I believe that I am going to... " The idea is to think about the situation, and tell recruiter how rational your thought and strategy would be, to deal with any given crisis. Your inexperience with a situation so far doesn't guarantee that you will never have to face it. It may surface anytime, while working in a team. Recruiter wants to know if you would be able to handle. Third advice: "Never duck from a situational question, even if you haven't faced it yet; imagine, think and answer."

- When you are asked to measure the weight of an airplane without using any scale - or to tell the number of light bulbs, recruiter's office building has? Questions can be many with varied answers. However, way to reckon your answer is just one - presence of mind! Global corporations, in a race to emerge as the best and most favored brand in their industry, are banking on the innovative products, services, and operational ideas. The company that comes up with a unique product or idea reaps the advantages of being an early bird. This has significantly altered the recruitment strategies; hence the recruiters' question banks too have changed, accordingly. Most candidates feel flabbergasted, when challenged by one of such weird questions. Remember that a recruiter is not a fool to have asked such a question. Through your reaction or answer, the inability or capability to think out of the box, perform in a high pressure environment, and ability to come up with an answer with trouble shooting attitude, are adjudged. Whatever your answer may be, recruiter is more focused on the way you derive the answer; the logical route that you treaded to reach that answer. Don't hesitate to request a minute to think, ask questions from recruiter to collect necessary data, and formulate your answer using a pen and a piece paper. Fourth advice: "Do whatever you can to find a logical answer, but don't panic!"

- A personal question, especially a non-relevant or illegal one, which you don't wish to answer - There is a whole list of questions that an interviewer has no right to ask, however, this doesn't proscribe some interviewers from asking such questions, intentionally or unintentionally. You could say, "Hey, you can't ask me that. That's illegal.", and that would succeed as well in refraining the interviewer from asking such questions, but at the end of the day, it might result in losing that job opportunity if the recruiter was pompous. So we have to adopt a way that gets us a 'safe exit'. You can start by saying, "I don't mind answering that question, however, I would first like to understand the objective behind asking this question, and perspective that the organization stands to gain through my answer." In all probabilities, the interviewer will understand what you intend to say, and revoke his question. Otherwise too, interviewer will have to give you a justification behind asking such question. Fifth advice: "Object to an illegal question, but in a way that interviewer feels neither offended, nor should be able to hold anything against you."

- When we are doubtful regarding the correctness of our answer - "Dilemma is to human mind" may not be a famous quote by someone big and well-known, however, it is a stark human reality. Usually, it happens because of incomplete information about a subject. It may also happen, when there is more than one school of thoughts existing for a subject. In case of an interview, there is a strong possibility that interviewer may not ratify the idea that we behold. Every interview has two aspects - technical and behavioral. There is no remedy for technical incompetence, however, for a behavioral ambiguity; it is always advisable to present your opinion, while simultaneously showing respect towards alternate theories. You can say, "The way I think is... , however, I am open for a heart to heart discussion with someone who believes otherwise." There you go! You told your perspective frankly, while showing your respect and acceptance for others' thoughts as well. Sixth advice: "Always present your opinion only. Don't give a verdict; respect other theories too."

- When we contradict one of our previous answers and get caught - A candidate applying for a sales job (which demanded a great deal of networking), when asked about his weakness, said, "I am a reserved kind of a person." Immediately, the next question catapulted at him was, "How do you do networking then?" Cat caught his tongue! The next step that he took, eliminated any chance for him to land in that job. He defended himself vehemently, and the interviewer, as his job demanded, kept digging. Soon, it became a heated argument, and you can all guess the outcome. What could he have done differently? First thing first! Accept that you made a blunder. To find an escape route is a rare opportunity in such situations. However, one can try to soothe the situation by presenting a different perspective, and smartly divert the topic. One could say, "I prefer to stay alone during my spare time, however, as far as professional networking is concerned, I am an adroit networker, with strong business links in this industry. My networking with over 500 industry professionals can easily be transformed into big business opportunity for the organization that I work for." Now, the interviewer would be more interested in exploring your contacts, and probable business avenues for the company. But the moment you start arguing and fighting, the game's over. In any situation, no matter what strategy you deploy, maintaining the poise in an awkward situation, and handling it with utmost diplomacy and presence of mind are the keys to success. Seventh advice: "If you've made a mistake, don't argue. It only makes matter worse."

If you believe that you handled the situation well, and still got rejected; don't hold up. Prepare for the next interview, because it's not the end of the journey.

Answer any interview question perfectly using the S.T.A.R. method**

Knowing what the interviewer wants to hear and being able to deliver the prefect answer gives you a huge advantage over any other candidates that will be interviewed.

✓ How to answer interview questions perfectly by using the S.T.A.R. method

Now on to the reason why we are here how to answer interview questions like an expert. You cannot answer questions with a yes or a no; you must always give real life examples. Give examples of challenges in you faced in your working life and then go on to describe how you overcame them. What you are about to read next will be the most important part of this guide take this with you into every interview situation The S.T.A.R. method

S.T.A.R. which stands for Situation, Task, Action, Result.

The S.T.A.R. method is a job interview technique used by interviewers to get all the pertinent information regarding a candidates specific capabilities that is needed for a particular job.

By following the S.T.A.R. method you will give a complete answers and present yourself in the best possible way that puts you a head of your competition. If executed correctly it can even make you look better then candidates that are more suited for the job!!!

✓ S.T.A.R Interview method step-by-step guide

The S.T.A.R Method has helped senior management to school leavers get the jobs they want. When you get asked: "Tell me about a time where you went above and beyond" or "when you made a great contribution" or "The thing you are most proud of in your career" or "a challenging situation that you overcame" or "when you worked well as a team" or "on your own"..and so and so forth you will answer using by using S.T.A.R. below I have broken down what it means.

S stands for Situation: You present a recent challenge and situation in which you found yourself.

T stands Task: What did you have to achieve? The interviewer will be looking to see what you were trying to achieve from the situation.

A stands for Action: What did you do? The interviewer will be looking for information on what you did, why you did it to achieve the task.

R stands for Results: What was the outcome of your actions? What did you achieve through your actions and did you meet your objectives? What did you learn from this experience and have you used this learning since?

✓ You start with SITUATION

"I had just taken over an existing project that was behind schedule"

"I was struggling to hit my first quarter targets I needed to win the sales completion"

✓ Move on to TASK

"I had just taken over an existing project that was behind schedule I needed to bring the project in on time or we could have lost a lot of money"

"I was struggling to hit my first quarter targets I needed to win the sales completion so that I could go an all expenses paid holiday"

✓ Then move to ACTION

"I had just taken over an existing project that was behind schedule I needed to bring the project in on time or we could have lost a lot of money so I arranged a meeting with rest of the team and my divisional manager and we rearranged priorities to concentrate resources on this key project and I worked 12 hour days until the project was completed"

"I was struggling to hit my first quarter targets I needed to win the sales completion so that I could go an all expenses paid holiday so I called all my existing clients that I sold to in the last 6 months and I made sure that I understood all new potential customer needs sold on the feature and benefits according to those needs"

✓ And finally Result

"I had just taken over an existing project that was behind schedule I needed to bring the project in on time or we could have lost a lot of money so I arranged a meeting with rest of the team and my divisional manager and we rearranged priorities to concentrate resources on this key project and I worked 12 hour days until the project was completed, this resulted in the project being handed over to the client before time making it even more profitable for the company as well as over achieving in the eyes of the client.

"I was struggling to hit my first quarter targets I needed to win the sales completion so that I could go an all expenses paid holiday so I called all my existing clients that I sold to in the last 6 months and I made sure that I understood all new potential customer needs I sold on the feature and benefits according to those needs, this resulted in me being the top sales person in the company by 15% and having the highest recorded sales revenue for the first quarter ever in the company history and taking my partner on an all expenses paid holiday to Hawaii"

Above are just two examples that may or may not fit your industry or situation, what is important is the S.T.A.R. method. Some interview question will be generic some will be very specific; however, it is vital that you think about scenarios that relate to your industry and work history and how to apply the S.T.A.R method. So remember the next time you are asked about a time when you had complete a task or how you solved a problem, start with the Situation then move onto the Task that needed to be completed follow that up with the Action you took to complete the task and finally move onto the Result. I hope this was helpful, good luck in your next job interview

Questions to Ask an Interviewer

A job interview tends to be a very one-sided affair. The interviewer asks you a number of interview questions and you try to answer these to the best of your ability.

However, generally near to the end of the job interview, a good interviewer should give you the opportunity to ask any questions that you may have about the job or the company. It is even more necessary that a candidate has questions to ask an interviewer if it is an Internet or telephone job interview, which is more likely if the employer is recruiting online.

As more and more companies are recruiting online the traditional form of face-to-face job interviews, which can involve the candidate traveling long distances, is becoming less prevalent. There are obvious benefits to this approach, such as the lower cost and the time saved for all parties but most importantly for job applicants, if you already have questions to ask an interviewer this gives you the opportunity, as it is an integral part of the communication process.

✓ So, what questions can you ask an interviewer?

Obviously, you need to prepare these properly before you are at the interview. Your questions need to be relevant to the job, the organization and your employer.

Avoid any questions that can be easily answered by a visit to the company's website or literature, as this could highlight that you have not completed any background research on the company before you the interview.

You should also be careful if you decide to ask about salary and related benefits at the first interview, as you do not want to give the impression that you are only interested in the financial aspects of the job instead of the job content.

This list of questions may be useful to you when you are preparing for a job interview:

1. What are the responsibilities in this position?

2. What areas will I have to give top priority to in the first month in the job?

3. Are there any immediate problems that need attending to?

4. How will my performance be measured?

5. What are the future promotion prospects in the company?

6. Is there any training for new employees?

7. How much authority will I be given to run the department?

8. What is the reputation of the department within the company?

9. What are the objectives for the department that I will be working in?

10. Can you give me a picture of the company's organizational structure?

11. What are the immediate goals of the company?

12. Do you perceive any threats that could affect jobs in the near future?

13. What is the key opportunity that the company is pursuing just now?

14. When are you aiming to make a decision?

15. If you offer me this job, what start date would you be aiming for?

You should definitely prepare some questions to ask an interviewer so that you will be more confident when go to the interview. You will not be able to ask all the questions so pick the ones that are most important to you and make sure you get the opportunity to ask them.

45 Common Behavioral Interview Questions

It has become a common practice for recruiters and hiring managers to ask behavioral interview questions. Behavioral interview questions allow them to use a candidate's past actions to predict their future behavior when facing certain issues/situations on the job. Below are listed 45 of the most commonly asked behavioral interview questions. By taking the time to review these common job interview questions, you will be better prepared for the interview because you will be able to apply true logic and provide evidence of your past accomplishments in your interview process. And these are the type of interviews that make difference in you getting the job or being passed over.

✓ ADAPTABILITY

1. Tell me about a situation in which you had to adjust to changes over which you had no control. How did you handle it?

2. Tell me about a time when you had to adjust to a colleague's working style in order to complete a project or achieve your objectives.

✓ ANALYTICAL SKILLS / PROBLEM SOLVING

3. What steps do you take to analyze a problem before making a decision? Why?

4. Tell me about a time when you had to analyze information and make a recommendation. What kind of thought process did you go through? Was the recommendation accepted? If not, why?

5. Tell me about a situation where you had to solve a difficult problem. What did you do? What was the outcome? What would you have had done differently?

✓ CUSTOMER SERVICE

6. When have you had to deal with an annoyed customer? What did you do? What was the end result?

7. Give an example of a time you went well out of your way to ensure a customer received the best possible service. What was their reaction?

✓ COMMUNICATION

8. Have you ever had to sell an idea to your co-workers? How did you do it?

9. Give me an example of a time when you were able to successfully communicate with another person even when that individual may not have personally liked you (or vice versa).

10. What obstacles or difficulties have you ever faced in communicating your ideas to a manager?

✓ CREATIVITY

11. Tell me about a problem that you've solved in a unique or unusual way. What was the outcome? Were you happy or satisfied with it?

12. When have you brought an innovative idea into your team? How was it received?

✓ DECISION MAKING

13. Tell me about a time when you had to make a decision without all the information you needed. How did you handle it?

14. Give me an example of a time when you had to be quick in coming to a decision. What obstacles did you face?

15. What is one the most difficult decision you've ever had to make at work? How did you arrive at your decision? What was the result?

16. Give me an example of a decision you made at work that you later regretted. What happened?

✓ GOAL SETTING

17. Give me an example of an important career goal which you set yourself and tell me how you reached it. What obstacles did you encounter? How did you overcome the obstacles?

18. Tell me about a professional goal that you set that you did not reach. How did it make you feel?

19. How have you gone about setting short-term goals and long-term goals for yourself or your team? What steps did you take along the way to keep yourself accountable?

✓ INITIATIVE

20. Describe a project or idea (not necessarily your own) that was implemented primarily because of your efforts. What was your role? What was the outcome?

21. Describe a situation in which you recognized a potential problem as an opportunity. What did you do? What was the result? What, if anything, do you wish you had done differently?

22. Tell me about a project you initiated. What did you do? Why? What was the outcome? Were you happy with the result?

23. Tell me about a time when your initiative caused a change to occur.

✓ INTERPERSONAL SKILLS

24. Give an example of when you had to work with someone who was difficult to get along with. How/why was this person difficult? How did you handle it? How did the relationship progress?

25. Describe a situation where you found yourself dealing with someone who didn't like you. How did you handle it?

26. Describe a recent unpopular decision you made. How was it received? How did you handle it?

27. What, in your opinion, are the key ingredients in guiding and maintaining successful professional relationships? Give me examples of how you have made these work for you.

28. Give me an example of a time when you were able to successfully communicate with another person even when that individual may not have personally liked you (or vice versa). How did you handle the situation?

✓ LEADERSHIP

29. Tell me about a team project when you had to take charge of the project? What did you do? What was the result?

30. Describe a leadership role of yours outside of work. Why did you commit your time to it? How did you feel about it?

31. What is the toughest group that you have ever had to lead? What were the obstacles? How did you handle the situation?

32. What has been your greatest leadership achievement in a professional environment? Talk through the steps you took to reach it.

33. What have been the greatest obstacles you have faced in building/growing a team?

34. Describe a time when you have not only been responsible for leading a team of people but for also doing the same job as your team members? How did you juggle/balance your time?

✓ PROJECT MANAGEMENT

35. Describe a situation that required you to do a number of things at the same time. How did you handle it? What was the result?

36. How do you prioritize projects and tasks when scheduling your time? Give me some examples.

37. Tell me about a project that you planned. How did your organize and schedule the tasks? Tell me about your action plan.

38. When has a project or event you organized not gone according to plan? What happened? Why? How did you feel?

✓ TEAMWORK

39. Describe a situation where others you were working with on a project disagreed with your ideas. What did you do?

40. Tell me about a time when you worked with a colleague who was not doing their share of the work. How did you handle it?

41. Describe a situation in which you had to arrive at a compromise or help others to compromise. What was your role? What steps did you take? What was the result?

42. Tell me about a time when you had to work on a team that did not get along. What happened? What role did you take? What was the result?

43. What was the biggest mistake you have made when delegating work as part of a team project?

44. Tell me about a time when you had to settle a dispute between team members. How did you go about identifying the issues? What was the result?

45. What have you found to be the difficult part of being a member, not leader, of a team? How did you handle this?

6 Common Teacher Interview Questions and How to Answer Them

When you get a call from a school administrator inviting you to interview for a teaching job, how do you feel? Happy? Elated? Excited? Nervous? Scared stiff?

You don't need to worry about the interview if you're a well-prepared, qualified candidate. Preparing for a teaching interview is a lot like studying for a test. You can review commonly asked questions, think about what you'll say beforehand, and go in to do your best. If you prepare beforehand, the interview questions will seem routine and familiar. You'll have answers on the tip of your tongue, ready-to-go.

Below is a list of six commonly asked teacher interview questions .How would you answer each question?

1. Tell us about yourself.

This will be the first question at almost every interview. Just give a brief background in about three sentences. Tell them what colleges you graduated from, what you're certified to teach, what your teaching & working experiences are, and why you'd love the job.

2. How do you teach to the state standards?

If you interview in the United States, school administrators love to talk about state, local, or national standards! Reassure your interviewer that everything you do ties into standards. Be sure the lesson plans in your portfolio have the state standards typed right on them. When they ask about them, pull out your lesson and show them the close ties between your teaching and the standards.

3. How will you prepare students for standardized assessments?

There are standardized assessments at almost every grade level. Be sure you know the names of the tests. Talk about your experiences preparing students. You'll get bonus points if you know and describe the format of the test because that will prove your familiarity.

4. Describe your discipline philosophy.

You use lots of positive reinforcement. You are firm, but you don't yell. You have appropriate consequences for inappropriate behavior. You have your classroom rules posted clearly on the walls. You set common routines that students follow. You adhere to the school's discipline guidelines. Also, emphasize that you suspect discipline problems will be minimal because your lessons are very interesting and engaging to students. Don't tell the interviewer that you "send kids to the principal's office" whenever there is a problem. You should be able to handle most discipline problems on your own. Only students who have committed very serious behavior problems should be sent to the office.

5. How do you make sure you meet the needs of a student with an IEP?

An IEP is an "individualized education plan." Students with special needs will be given an IEP, or a list of things that you must do when teaching the child. An IEP might include anything from "additional time for testing" to "needs all test questions read aloud" to "needs to use braille textbook." How do you ensure you're meeting the needs of a student with an IEP? First, read the IEP carefully. If you have questions, consult a special education teacher, counselor, or other staff member who can help you. Then, you just make sure you follow the requirements on the IEP word for word. When necessary, you may be asked to attend a meeting in which you can make suggestions for updating the IEP. Your goal, and the goal of the IEP, is to make sure the student has whatever he or she needs to be successful in your class.

6. How do you communicate with parents?

This question will come up at almost every elementary school interview. It's fairly common in the middle school and high school as well. You might have a weekly parent newsletter that you send home each week. For grades 3 and up, you may require students to have an assignment book that has to be signed each night. This way, parents know what assignments are given and when projects are due. When there are discipline problems you call home and talk to parents. It's important to have an open-door policy and invite parents to share their concerns at any time.

Interview Bloopers And How To Correct Them

I'm sure you've sat through movie or TV "bloopers" at the end of shows and laughed at the mistakes the actors make during the filming of the show. If I could put together a film with bloopers that people make in interviews it might seem funny as well - but not when it happens in real life - to you!

How do you avoid bloopers? First you become aware of what some of the pitfalls of interviewing are and then you prepare and practice so that it won't happen to you. Here are 10 of those very pitfalls to watch for.

1. Poor non-verbal communication - slouching - fidgeting - lack of eye contact

It's about demonstrating confidence - standing straight, making eye contact, and connecting with a good, firm handshake. That first impression can be a great beginning, or a quick ending to your interview.

2. Not dressing for the job or company - "over casual"

Today's casual dress codes in the office, do not give you permission to dress as "they" do when you interview. It is important to look professional and well groomed, above all. Whether you wear a suit or something less formal depends on the company culture and the position you are seeking. If possible, call and find out what the company dress code is before the interview.

3. Not listening - only worrying about what you are going to say

From the very beginning of the interview, your interviewer is giving you information, either directly or indirectly. If you are not listening - turning up your intuitive - you are missing a major opportunity. Good communication skills include listening and letting the person know you heard what they said. Observe your interviewer and match that style and pace.

4. Talking too much - telling it all - even if it's not relevant

Telling the interviewer more than they need to know could be a fatal mistake. When you have not prepared ahead of time you may tend to ramble, sometimes talking yourself right out of the job. Prepare for the interview by reading through the job posting; matching your skills with the requirements of the position, and relating only that information.

5. Being over-familiar - your new best friend is NOT the interviewer

The interview is a professional meeting to talk business. This is not about making a new friend. The level of familiarity should mimic the demeanor of the interviewer. It is important to bring energy and enthusiasm to the interview, and to ask questions, but not to over-step your place as a candidate looking for a job.

6. Using inappropriate language - you "guys" know what I mean

It's a given that you should use professional language during the interview. Be aware of any inappropriate slang words or references to age, race, religion, politics, or sexual preferences - these topics could get the door slammed very quickly.

7. Acting cocky - being overconfident - "king of the hill"

Attitude plays a key role in your interview success. There is a fine balance between confidence, professionalism, and modesty. Even if you're putting on a performance to demonstrate your ability, over-doing is as bad, if not worse, as being too reserved.

8. Not answering the question asked - "jumping in without thinking"

When an interviewer asks for an "example of a time," you did something, he is seeking a sample of your past behavior. If you fail to relate a "specific" example, you not only don't answer the question, but you miss an opportunity to prove your ability and tell about your skills.

9. Not asking questions - a missed opportunity you will live to regret

When asked if they have any questions, the majority of candidates answer, "No." Wrong answer! It is extremely important to ask questions. It demonstrates an interest in what goes on in the company. It also gives you the opportunity to find out if this is the right place for you. The best questions come from listening to what is asked during the interview, and asking for additional information.

10. Appearing desperate - "Please, please hire me!"

It's a tough job market, and you need a job! But, when you interview with the "Please, please, hire me," approach you appear desperate and less confident. Maintain the three "C's" during the interview: Cool, Calm, and Confident! You know you can do the job, - now, make sure the interviewer believes you can, too.

Everybody makes mistakes - that's what makes us human. We can laugh at ourselves a great deal of the time when we get tongue-tied or forget someone's name - even our spouse's. But in the interview you want to be as prepared and polished as possible. If you do make a mistake, consider it a human error and learn from the experience. In the meantime do your homework and get prepared.

Pharmaceutical Sales Interview Questions - How To Answer Behavioral Questions Like a Pharma Pro

Pharmaceutical sales interview questions are typically situational (behavioral) in nature. These techniques are based on the premise that past behavior is a great indicator of future behavior. Therefore, all behavioral interview questions ask you to provide examples of real life occurrences that illustrate a particular skill or ability, as in organization, teamwork, persuasion, sales ability, tenaciousness, etc.

These questions usually begin with any of the following:

- Tell me about a time when...
- Give me an example where...
- Describe a situation where...

This is your alert to answer the question by providing a real life example.

However, there's more to it than just telling your story...it needs to be logical, concise, and clearly illustrate that you posses the skill/ability in question. Enter...the STAR format! What's that, you ask? Well my friend, it's a format you can use to help answer the question in a logical, sequential, understandable manner!

✓ The basic components of the STAR format:

Situation: What was the situation you found yourself in? Provide necessary background information.

Task: What was the specific task you had to achieve? What was the goal?

Action: What action did you take? How did you create the solution and what did you do?

Result: What was the result of your action? What happened?

Let's try an example, shall we?

Interviewer: "Tell me about a time where you used negotiation skills to affect your company's bottom line?"

Candidate's Response:

Situation: "As a franchise owner and operator, I was constantly looking for new ways in which to grow my business. By my 2nd year in business, my referral system was kicking in nicely, but I really wanted to double the year's previous earnings.

Task: I knew in order to double company earnings, I'd have to contract with commercial businesses - where the "big money" can be made. Living in a college town, I knew it would be wise to focus on the larger real estate companies in town - specifically those that managed many large apartment complexes.

Action: I utilized industry contacts and scheduled an appointment with the largest realty company in town, which also owned the most apartment complexes. After assessing their needs and goals, I constructed a business plan and negotiated a win-win situation for all of us. I agreed to take on many of the administrative tasks of yearly move- outs; they were thrilled at my offer. I then explained the features and benefits of our extensive cleaning services that related to their current needs. The end-result of my negotiation? We now had a yearly contract - which meant a stable income, plus they agreed to pay $5/more per hour than they originally quoted.

Result: As a result of that one commercial account, my business earnings more that doubled and the referrals I earned from my negotiations paid off for several years down the road!

Notice the logical progression of this example? Is there any doubt that this candidate possesses negotiation skills? No! In addition, organizing your answers in the STAR format shows exceptional communication skills as you clearly and effortlessly lead the interviewer through the situation, task, action and result.

As I've mentioned time and time again in our Pharmaceutical Sales Interview Coaching Blog, Preparation is the Key to Successful Pharma Sales Interviews. With that being said, how should you prepare for a behavioral interview?

The Importance of Note Taking in Interviewing

Note taking is absolutely paramount when conducting an interview. The notes you take will be the only way to verify the facts garnered in the interview. Relying solely on memory will lead to thinking only about impressions. This leads to biases and preconceptions. Whether we realize it or not, everyone has developed biases and even if they are subconscious they can affect the way we view a candidate. Interviewing is more than a gut feeling, it's about finding the best person who has the knowledge, ability and experience to do the job. Note taking is imperative for successful hiring.

When you conduct an interview, let the candidate know up front that you will be taking notes. If you have planned properly, all of your questions have been prepared and you have a space underneath each question to fill in with notes. Give the candidate plenty of time to answer the questions and make sure that you redirect and clarify when necessary. Your notes will help you with this. Proper preparation and good note taking will help you collect more complete and accurate information.

As you take your notes, be very careful to stick to the facts. Making inferences or judgments will do you no good when you go to review your notes after the interview. Great interviewing is about facts. It's about finding out about past behaviors so that you can predict how the candidate will handle future situations. Objectivity is the key.

When the interview is finished, review your notes immediately. Never do interviews back to back. Allow at least 15-20 minutes between interviews for review. When an interview is finished, it is fresh in your mind and you will be able to effectively and objectively review the information - the more time that goes by, the better the chance that you will use impressions rather than facts in your decision. This review period is also a good time to make sure you received all the information you needed. If you missed something, it can be immediately set up for a future interview or by a phone follow-up.

When you sit down with colleagues later to give your input on the candidate, you will be able to present them with the objective facts. If they also interviewed the candidate or if you did a team interview, it will be easy to compare notes and make an objective decision.

Note taking is imperative in the interviewing process. We simply can't be expected to remember everything said in an interview and if we try our decisions will be at least partially based on gut feelings and biases. Note taking leads to successful and productive interviews and as a result to successful and productive employees.

Different Types of Second Interview Questions That You Should Be Familiar With

Congratulations, you have passed your first interview and are ready to move on to the next step, the second interview. This interview is generally more in-depth than the first and brings you one step closer to getting hired. In order for the interview to go smoothly you need to be prepared to answer any questions that be asked in the interview process.

The second interview questions are often similar to the initial interview questions. Because of this try to remember the questions you may have had difficulty answering during the first interview and practice new and improved answers. However, often the second interview questions are new and more difficult to answer than the first because the interviewers are really trying to get a good idea of who they are hiring and therefore may ask harder questions. Some of the possible types of questions you may be asked to answer are as follows:

✓ Open Questions. This type of question deals with your strength and personality by asking you to contribute a long answer. They usually begin with the interviewer asking you to tell them about a particular time in your educational or employment history. These questions are best answered by highlighting your strength and skills and remember that it is not wise to answer the question by stating your weaknesses and limitation.

✓ Closed Questions. Closed questions are generally answerable with a simple yes or no. However, in some instances, interviewers will ask for specific and factual information when you answer the question.

✓ Behavioral Questions. These questions try to forecast your future behavior based from your past experience. When answering this type of question, state your past experience by focusing on how you have developed your skills.

✓ Hypothetical Questions. Typically, this kind of question is one that forces you to think deeply. Generally, it is asked in a form of a "what if" question. The purpose of this type of questions is to assess your capability to think immediately, and provide a thoughtful answer.

In general these questions are usually more focused on your personality and technical skills so be sure to respond to the questions consistently. In addition, try to tailor your answer in such a way that the interviewer will like the way you answer the question. Your first interview was a success, that's why you got the second interview so study hard and be prepared to ace it with these great tips .

Army Officer Interview Questions And Answers

Many people attend the Army Officer interview but only a small percentage succeed. The reason for this is simply because they fail to provide sufficient evidence of their 'officer' potential. You are guaranteed to get asked the following question during the Army Officer interview:

✓ Can you tell me why you want to become an Officer?

You must have valid reasons why you want to become an Officer in the Army. This job is entirely different to being a regular soldier. You will have far more responsibilities and the training that you will undergo will be extremely challenging, both mentally and physically. Here are a few positive reasons for wanting to become an Officer:

"An opportunity to become an elite Officer in the Army is an opportunity to be the best that I can be."

"I believe that I have the potential to become an exceptional Officer and I don't want to waste my potential."

"I want to become an Officer simply because I believe I have the skills and attributes to lead, inspire and develop people. If I am not in a leadership position then I believe those skills and attributes will be wasted."

"I am a confident, professional and enthusiastic person who believes that everyone should be given the opportunity to be there best. As an Officer I would have the chance to make a difference and I would thrive in a position that could help the Army to achieve its organizational goals and objectives."

"In any organisation that I have worked in so far, I have always held a keen interest in the development of staff and the development of the company as a whole. The experiences that I have gained in life so far and prepared me to become an Officer in the Army and I believe that I could be a excellent member of the Army's leadership team."

If you use any of the above reasons for wanting to become an army officer you will have more chances of success.

INTERVIEW TIPS FOR THE ARMY OFFICER INTERVIEW

- When you walk into the interview room stand up straight with your shoulders back. Project an image of confidence;

- Don't sit down in the interview chair until invited to do so;

- Sit with your hands resting on your knees, palms downwards. It is OK to use your hands expressively but don't overdo it;

- Don't slouch in the chair;

- Speak up and be positive;

- Smile, be happy and have a sense of humour;

- Dress as smart as you can and take a pride in your appearance. If you don't have a suit make sure you wear a shirt and tie at the very least.

- Improve your personal administration. By this I mean your personal hygiene and cleanliness. Make sure you have washed and your hands and nails are clean.

- Make sure you have researched both the Army life and your chosen career/careers. This is very important.

- During the interview do not be negative or disrespectful towards your teachers, parents or people in positions of authority. Remember that you are applying to join a disciplined service.

- Go the extra mile and learn a little bit about the Army's history if you get time. When the panel asks you 'What can you tell us about the Army?' you will be able to demonstrate that you have made an effort to look into their history as well as their modern day activities;

- Be respectful and courteous towards the interview panel. At the end of your response to each question finish off with either 'Sir' or 'Ma'am' or as otherwise instructed.

- Ask positive questions at the end of the interview. Try not to ask questions such as "How much leave will I get?" or "How often do I get paid?"

- If you are unsure about a question don't waffle. If you do not know the answer then it is OK to say so. Move on to the next question and put it behind you.

How to Handle Tricky Interview Questions

Interviewers use tricky questions to weed out people who can't handle stressful situations correctly. Many candidates often prepare responses prior to the interview, including researching the company before hand, building a solid resume and skills sheet, and getting quality references to prove who you say you are. The problem is that for many people they don't often think about the questions that interviewers can possibly ask during an interview. Here are some questions that most people can't respond correctly on:

✓ Can you give an example from a previous job where you failed to meet an objective.

The reason why many people fail this question, it's because they don't know how to answer it without saying something negative about themselves. Just remember that when answering this question, realize that everybody, including the interviewer, has failed at some point at their career. Don't try to cover up the fact that you did something wrong in your career. Definitely don't say that you've never failed to meet your signed objective, because that just shows that you are cocky and arrogant. Some job interviewers just want to know that you can tell the truth, and don't really care about the answer to the question. Try to describe third-party obstacles that hindered performance of the task. Be sure not to make your explanation sound like an excuse for poor performance, and definitely don't blame something on another person. Describe a situation where you felt because of something that you couldn't control, and the interviewer can understand where you're coming from.

✓ Describe a situation where your work has been criticized negatively.

Just like with the previous question, nobody's perfect, and you probably have made a mistake sometime in your career. Just remember to be honest, be confident, and be thorough with your answer. Think about one answer prior to the interview that you can remember to talk about during the interview, so you don't get blindsided with this question. In your response, mention how you are able to deal with this criticism, and how you improved your work after the criticism came about.

✓ What have you learned from your mistakes?

A successful career doesn't necessarily mean you make the most money, it means that you've transformed from the day you started to the current day. Learning from your mistakes, and other people's mistakes is vital to improving your job performance. Your job interviewer wants to know that you can come back from a bad mistake, and make your future performance better for everybody around you. Think of examples that positively demonstrate healthy workplace environments. Be sure to be specific, but also be brief in your answer.

What Are Your Weaknesses? - The Interview Question Answered

One of the most challenging questions in a job interview is 'What are your weaknesses?'. Many write ups that suggest ways to answer this question conflict with each other. Here are some tips that will help you answer this question without compromising your chance of getting that job.

There can be two purposes for this question:

1. The interviewer wants to check how well you can think of your own.

2. The interviewer really wants to know what your weakness is because it is a part of his job.

There is an old approach to answering this question, which is a big no-no: Trying to find something that is really an asset and mentioning it as a weakness. This is wrong! Stop doing this in your interviews.

For example, you may say that you work really hard and explain it as if it were a weakness. This is cheating and a lot of interviewers may not like it. When the interviewer asks for your weakness, he actually wants you to talk about your weakness and not try to hide it.

But this is a very tricky situation. What if you don't get the job just because you uncovered a weakness that is really not a weakness to have for the kind of job you are applying for?

For example, when you are attending an interview for a customer support executive position, you may not want to say that you are not good in developing a rapport with people. It is essential for a customer support executive to develop rapport with customers, because no one would want to talk to a boring, reserved or rude guy over the phone.

Another big mistake that people make while answering this question is saying that they don't have any weaknesses. Anyone can say that you are lying, when you give such a reply to this question. No one is perfect and it is human to have some weaknesses. It is absolutely OK for a person to have a weakness as long as he or she is doing something to overcome it.

✓ Here are the steps involved in coming up with a good answer to this question:
   - Take some time and dig deep inside yourself. Do an honest self-assessment and make a note of all your weaknesses.
   - Strike off the weaknesses that can compromise your chance of getting that interview. You do want to be honest but that doesn't mean you have to reveal everything that is bad about you.

- Once you pick a weakness which is OK to reveal, think about what you are doing to overcome it. If you are not doing anything to overcome it, then you better start doing something right away.
- Mention this weakness in the interview as the answer to the question 'What are your weaknesses?'. Explain what you are trying to do to overcome it and how you dealt with situations in the past that challenged this weakness.
- Your honest reply regarding your weakness and your sincere attempt to overcome it will definitely impress your interviewer. When you go for your next interview, make sure you don't do the mistakes we talked about.

Conclusion

There are countless questions that you may be asked in an interview, so many that it's really impossible to guess which ones you'll be faced with. Instead, you should realize that the key to how to answer interview questions lies more in your attitude than in your answers.Confidence, creativity, and a positive attitude are more often than not exactly what employers are on the lookout for and as long as you can answer your interview questions with these factors in mind you should have nothing to worry about in the least.

© *Written By : Ernest Enabulele*

About The Author

Ernest Enabulele is a bestselling author, interview coach and CV consultant based in London, England and brings an infectious enthusiasm and a tremendous nine years' experience to his books.

His problem-solving persona has helped him see more possibilities of how he could be of help to those who look forward to acing an interview. After coming across several job applicants struggling to ace their interview, he innovated the series of books, 'How To Be Successful At Interview' in July 2018 and "Interview Preparation And Success Tips" in December 2018.

Having worked with people across multiple industries, in both private and public sectors, Ernest knows first-hand what it takes to get hired in a competitive job market -- and would love to help job seekers do the same. Interestingly, his books not only include details of how to sell yourself at interviews but also provide samples, most likely traditional and competency based interview questions & answers to expect during interviews.

In his career years, he has successfully helped a range of job seekers get the jobs or promotions they desire. Now he wants to help you do the same. He is passionate about helping clients achieve their goals -- he has worked with talented professionals from all over the world who succeeded in getting job offers in very competitive fields.

Ernest is here to help you understand what your unique selling points are and what value you can bring to an organization. He has authored several books, many of which were written in conjunction with people currently serving in that particular field.

His goal is to help job-seekers gain more opportunities and also expand the reach of their business. Therefore, his books are written from a desire to help job-seekers land the job of their dreams, achieve their goals.

The 'How To Be Successful At Interviews' and Interview Preparation and Success Tips: A Detailed Guide on How to Answer Interview Questions and Bag That Dream Job series are inspiring and an excellent guide to interviews. It is his passion to help you be at ease, engaging, and confident when talking to others about your talents, skills, and qualifications.

His bestselling self-help books for job-seekers include:

• Interview Preparation and Success Tips: A Detailed Guide on How to Answer Interview Questions and Bag That Dream Job!

• How to Be Successful at Interviews: An In-Depth Guide on Interviewing, Answering Questions, and Putting Your Best Foot Forward

• Effective Interview Tips: Tested strategies for a successful job interview

For more information :

Go to www.cvinterviewservices.com

www.ernestenabulele.com

cvinterviewservices@mail.com

ernestenabulele@mail.com

Printed in Great Britain
by Amazon

55852020R00077